SPACE EXPLORERS

SPACECRAFT

by Jenny Fretland VanVoorst

pogo

Ideas for Parents and Teachers

Pogo Books let children practice reading informational text while introducing them to nonfiction features such as headings, labels, sidebars, maps, and diagrams, as well as a table of contents, glossary, and index.

Carefully leveled text with a strong photo match offers early fluent readers the support they need to succeed.

Before Reading

- "Walk" through the book and point out the various nonfiction features. Ask the student what purpose each feature serves.
- Look at the glossary together. Read and discuss the words.

Read the Book

- Have the child read the book independently.
- Invite him or her to list questions that arise from reading.

After Reading

- Discuss the child's questions. Talk about how he or she might find answers to those questions.
- Prompt the child to think more. Ask: Were you familiar with any of the spacecraft mentioned in this book? Which ones? Which spacecraft would you like to learn more about?

Pogo Books are published by Jump!
5357 Penn Avenue South
Minneapolis, MN 55419
www.jumplibrary.com

Library of Congress Cataloging-in-Publication Data

Names: Fretland VanVoorst, Jenny, 1972- author.
Title: Spacecraft / by Jenny Fretland VanVoorst.
Description: Minneapolis, MN: Jump!, Inc. [2016]
Series: Space explorers: Audience: Age 7-10.
Includes bibliographical references and index.
Identifiers: LCCN 2016024524 (print)
LCCN 2016025127 (ebook)
ISBN 9781620314166 (hardcover: alk. paper)
ISBN 9781624964633 (ebook)
Subjects: LCSH: Space vehicles–Juvenile literature.
Space flight–Juvenile literature.
Aerospace engineering–Juvenile literature.
Classification: LCC TL795 .F74 2016 (print)
LCC TL795 (ebook) | DDC 629.47–dc23
LC record available at https://lccn.loc.gov/2016024524

Editor: Kirsten Chang
Series Designer: Anna Peterson
Book Designer: Leah Sanders
Photo Researcher: Anna Peterson

Photo Credits: Alamy, 8-9, 20, 21; Getty, 4, 12, 13, 18-19, 23; NASA, 16-17; Science Source Images, cover, 6-7; Shutterstock, 1, 5, 10-11, 14-15; wws001/Shutterstock.com, 3.

Printed in the United States of America at Corporate Graphics in North Mankato, Minnesota.

TABLE OF CONTENTS

CHAPTER 1

MAN UP!

Rockets blast into space. **Rovers** collect Mars rock. **Space stations** house **astronauts** at work.

Space **probes** explore the **solar system** and beyond. All are spacecraft.

Some support human travel. They are manned spacecraft.

Manned space travel began in 1961. **Soviet cosmonaut** Yuri Gagarin **orbited** the planet in *Vostok 1*. Then he fell safely back to Earth.

DID YOU KNOW?

How do spacecraft get into space? They are launched by rockets!

Vostok 1

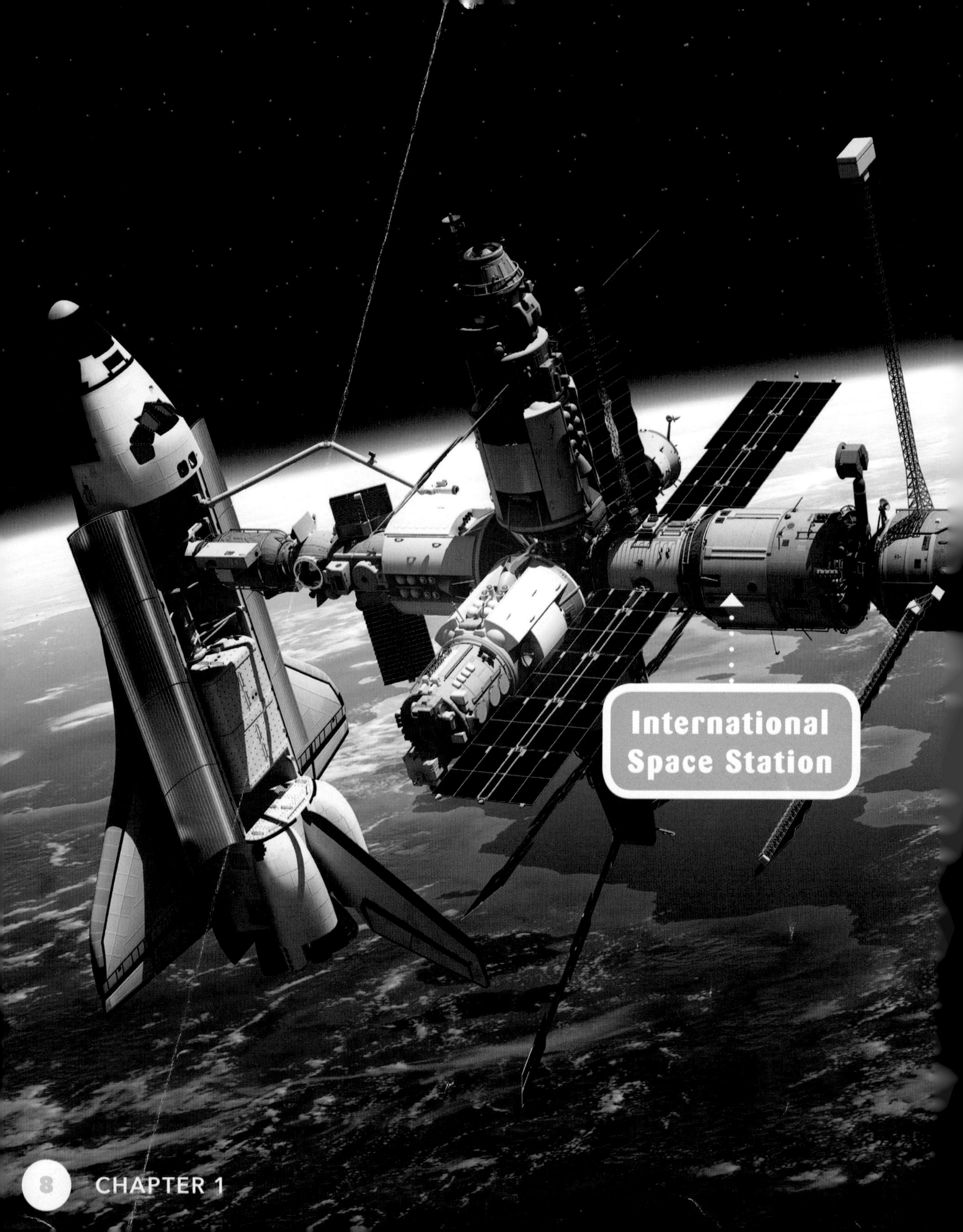
International
Space Station

The space shuttle was one of the most successful spacecraft of all time. Its first flight was in 1981. It sent people and supplies to space stations.

DID YOU KNOW?

To date, only three nations have flown manned spacecraft. Which ones? China. The United States. The Soviet Union (now Russia).

The space shuttle made 135 trips. It was retired in 2011. Why? The vehicles were growing old. They were expensive, too. Each flight cost more than a billion dollars!

DID YOU KNOW?

The first space shuttle was *Columbia*. It flew 28 missions over 22 years. It broke apart during re-entry in 2003. All seven crew members were killed.

CHAPTER 2

NO PILOT? NO PROBLEM!

Most spacecraft are unmanned. Some are **autonomous** robots. Others are remote-controlled.

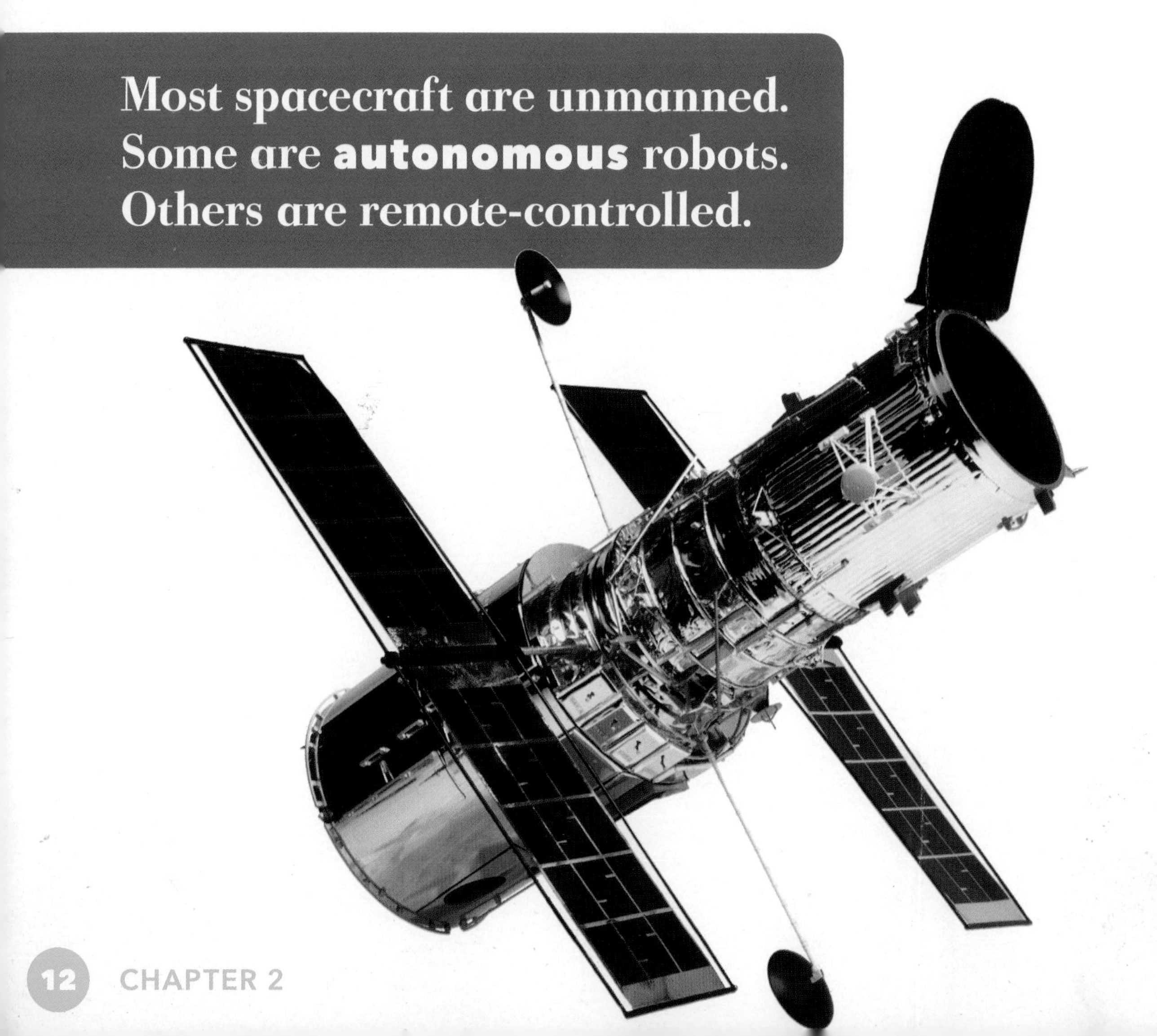

Most early missions are **flybys**. The spacecraft passes close to a planet or moon. It takes pictures on its way past.

Curiosity
(Mars rover)

To learn more, spacecraft orbit the planet. They do long-term, in-depth studies.

Eventually, one might land on the planet's surface. Rovers on Mars travel the planet's hills and valleys. They study rocks and soil.

Unmanned spacecraft have visited every planet in our solar system. They have sent us pictures from as far away as Pluto.

TAKE A LOOK!

Here are a few of the most successful recent missions:

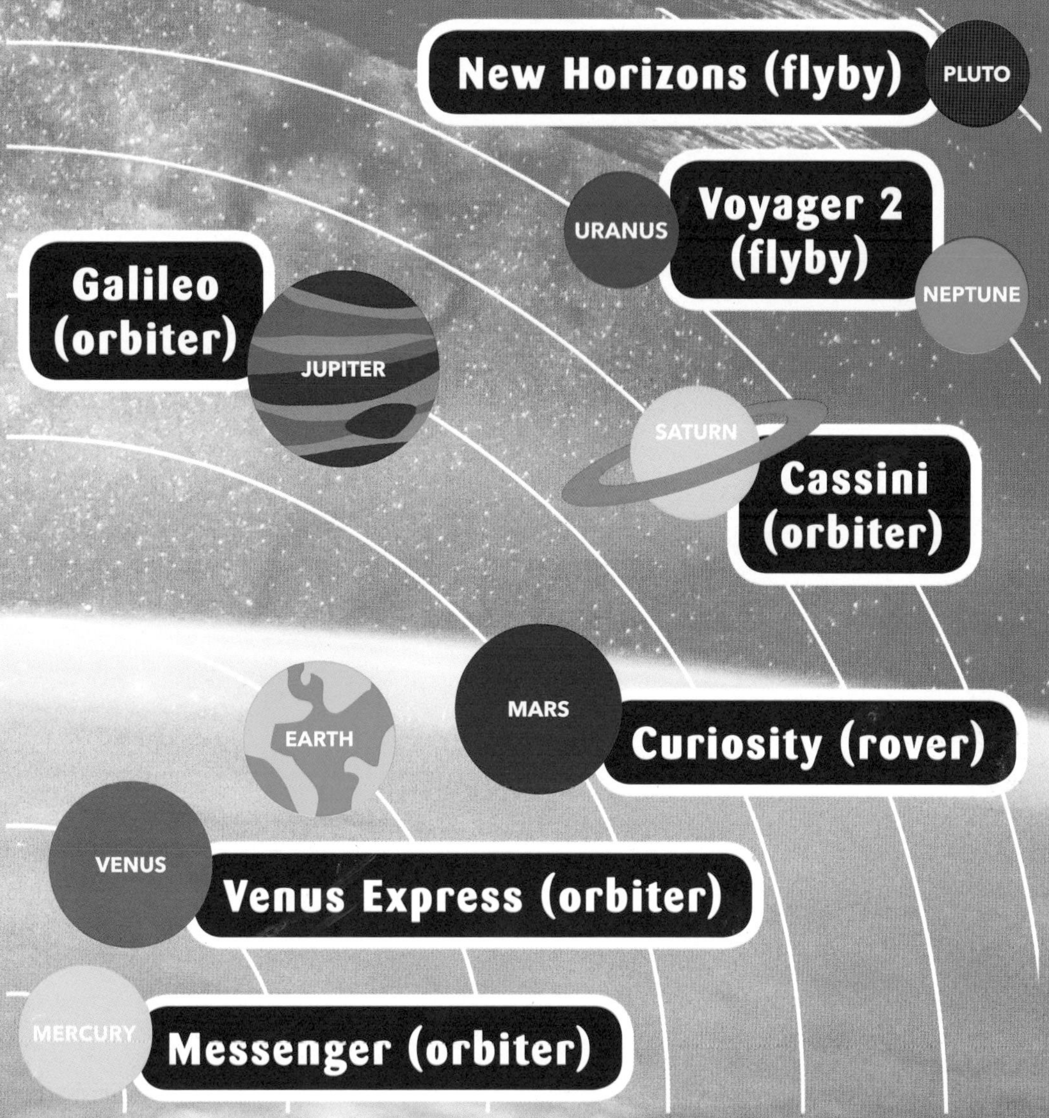

New Horizons (flyby) — PLUTO

Voyager 2 (flyby) — URANUS, NEPTUNE

Galileo (orbiter) — JUPITER

Cassini (orbiter) — SATURN

Curiosity (rover) — MARS

EARTH

Venus Express (orbiter) — VENUS

Messenger (orbiter) — MERCURY

Most spacecraft stay in our solar system. But some have a different mission. At least three spacecraft are on paths that lead beyond the reach of our sun. Who knows what they will find?

CHAPTER 3

THE FUTURE

Exploring space is expensive. Most missions have been led by large governments. But the future of space travel may look very different.

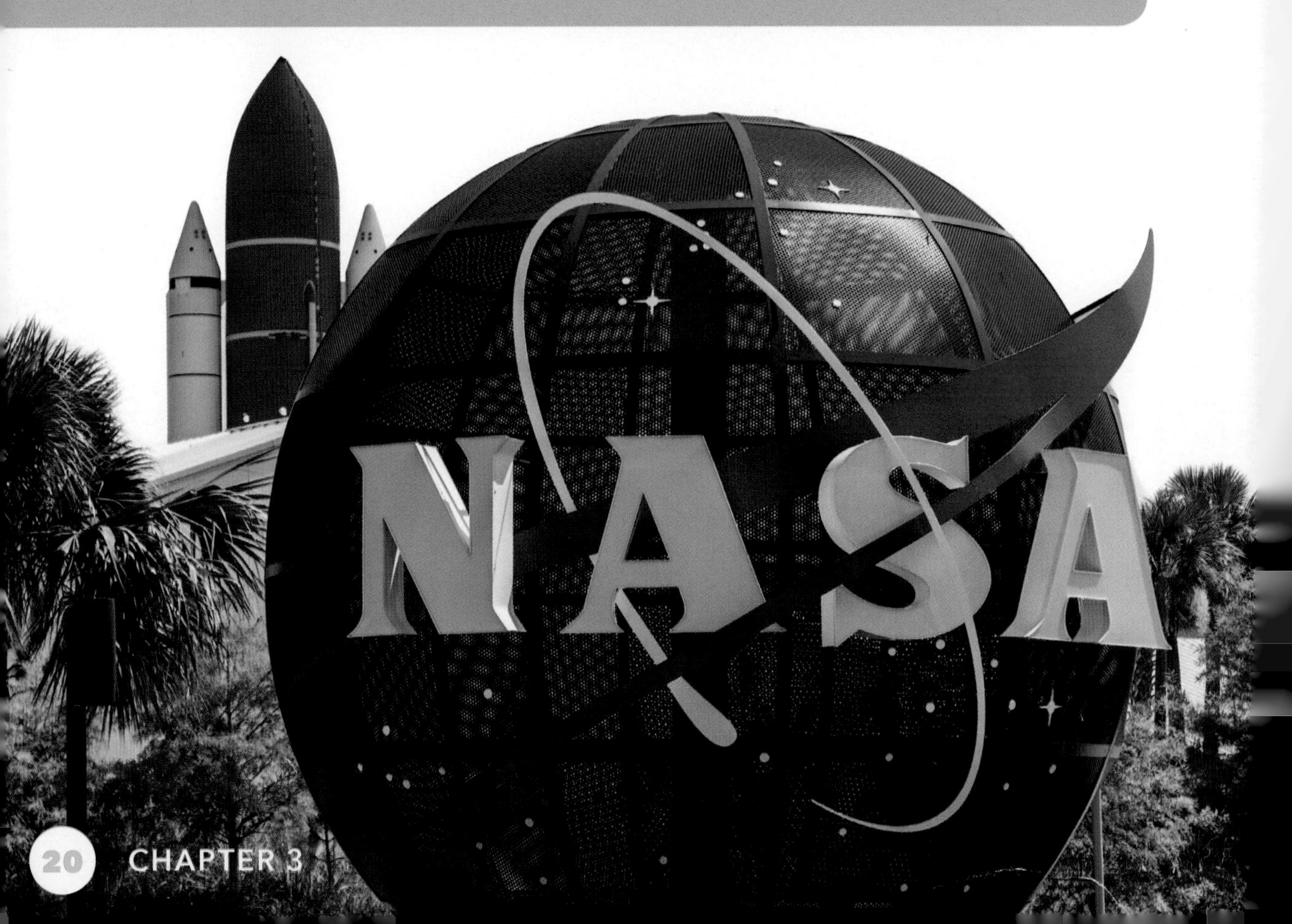

It is more likely to be led by private companies. Private citizens, too, are reaching for the stars! Where do you think we will travel next? Would you like to play a part?

ACTIVITIES & TOOLS

TRY THIS!

EXPLORE A SPACECRAFT

In this activity, you will use the Internet to learn more about a spacecraft. If you need help using the Internet, ask an adult.

Is there a spacecraft that holds particular interest for you? How about a planet? Choose a spacecraft associated with that planet, or pick one mentioned in this book. Learn everything you can about your spacecraft. Answer the following questions:

1. **What is your spacecraft called?**
2. **What is or was its mission?**
3. **What country or countries is/are responsible for its mission?**
4. **When was it launched? Is it still operational?**
5. **What are some of the characteristics of the spacecraft?**
6. **What discoveries has it made?**

GLOSSARY

astronauts: People who have been trained to fly aboard a spacecraft and work in space.

autonomous: Able to make certain decisions without human input.

cosmonaut: The name Russians use for their astronauts.

flybys: When spacecraft travel past a planet in order to take photos but do not orbit or land.

orbit: To travel in a fixed path around a planet or other object in space.

probes: Space exploration vehicles.

rockets: Space vehicles that are driven through the air by the gases produced by a burning substance.

rovers: Spacecraft that travel over a planet's surface in order to conduct experiments.

solar system: The planets that, along with Earth, revolve around our sun.

Soviet: Belonging to the Soviet Union, a large country in eastern Europe and western Asia that broke apart in 1991; Russia was once part of the Soviet Union and now runs its space program.

space stations: Places where astronauts live and work in space.

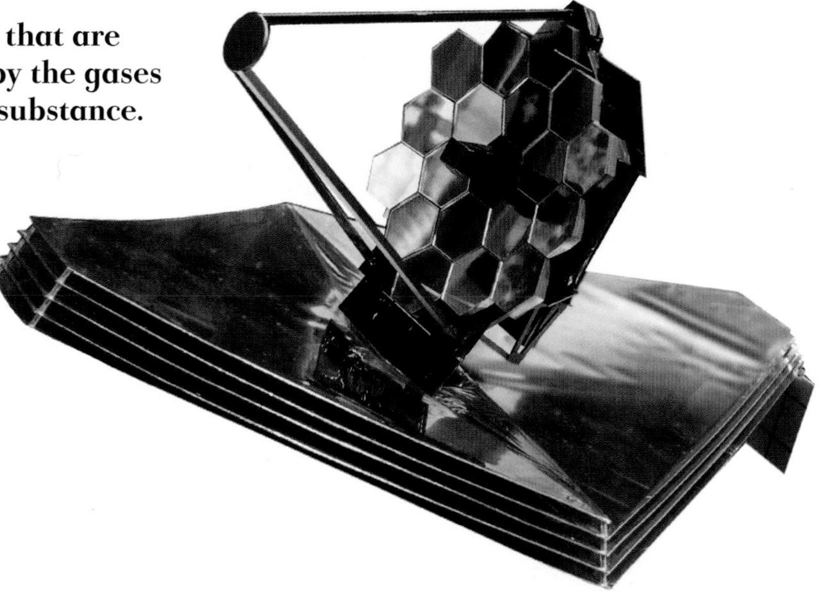

INDEX

TO LEARN MORE

Learning more is as easy as 1, 2, 3.

1) Go to www.factsurfer.com
2) Enter "spacecraft" into the search box.
3) Click the "Surf" button to see a list of websites.

With factsurfer, finding more information is just a click away.